INDUS VALLEY CIVILIZATION

A History from Beginning to End

Copyright © 2019 by Hourly History.

All rights reserved.

Table of Contents

Introduction
Discovery
Excavation of Harappa
Origins
Early Harappan Phase: 3300 to 2600 BCE
Life and Death in the Indus Valley
Mature Harappan Phase: 2600 to 1900 BCE
Late Harappan Phase: 1900 to 1300 BCE
Downfall of the Indus Valley Civilization
Conclusion

Introduction

The Indus Valley Civilization was one of the largest ancient civilizations. At its peak, it included more than five million inhabitants and covered an area which was greater than Ancient Egypt and Mesopotamia combined. However, perhaps the most surprising thing about this culture is that, one hundred years ago, no-one even suspected it had ever existed.

Victorian British railway builders working in present-day India were the first to discover the remains of large cities in the Punjab, but it wasn't until the 1920s that there was a concerted attempt to undertake an archaeological examination of these places. What emerged were the remains of a vast culture which was one of the most advanced in the ancient world.

The Indus Valley Civilization created cities 4,000 years ago which were carefully planned and had more than 30,000 occupants who lived in homes that featured baths and flush toilets. However, all the excavation of sites belonging to this culture (more than 1,000 have been identified so far) have failed to find some significant components. This society created no palaces or large temples for example, and no-one has found any evidence of armor or shields or the kind of equipment normally associated with armies. It seems that this was a peaceful, egalitarian society which was not ruled by a king or emperor and which expanded and controlled territory without armies or conquests.

These factors make the Indus Valley Civilization fascinating, but there is still a great deal we don't know about this culture. Although it was one of the first ancient civilizations to develop a system of writing, their texts have not been deciphered so we know little about the structure and organization of their society. However, perhaps the greatest mystery about the Indus Valley Civilization was what happened to cause it to disappear. There are a number of theories, but none seem to fit all the known facts.

We are still learning about this advanced ancient culture, but this is what we know so far about the mysterious Indus Valley Civilization.

Chapter One

Discovery

"I was much exercised in my mind how we were to get ballast for the line of the railway."

—John Brunton

In 1856, workers were constructing what would become the Punjab Railway, one of the first railways in the British colony of India connecting the cities of Lahore and Karachi in present-day Pakistan. The indigenous workers, supervised by British engineers John and William Brunton, were digging out the foundations on the Multan-Lahore section of the track when they discovered thousands of fire-baked mud bricks buried in the dusty earth. The British engineers were delighted—there was a shortage of material in the local area which was suitable to use as ballast for the track bed, and these bricks were ideal. However, the engineers wondered just where these bricks, which were obviously ancient, had originally come from.

On another section of track, near the village of Harappa, the new line once again passed what appeared to be ruins, and again the bricks discovered buried in the ground were used as ballast for the track. William Brunton later wrote, "A section of the line ran near another ruined city, bricks from which had already been used by villagers in the nearby village of Harappa at the same site. These bricks now provided ballast along 93 miles of the railroad track running from Karachi to Lahore."

These bricks were not just a useful source of building material; they also indicated the existence of large, unknown ruins in this area. This was not the first time that these remains had been examined by an outsider—in the 1830s, an explorer and soldier of the British East India Company, James Lewis (who wrote under the pseudonym Charles Masson), had discovered several brick mounds and apparent ruins near the city of Sahiwal in Punjab, around 150 kilometers (93 miles) from Lahore. No-one seemed to be sure just who had created the buildings which formed these ruins. Local people spoke of an ancient city called Brahminabad which, they said, had covered more than "13 cosses" (around 40 kilometers or 25 miles), but the only people who were known to have lived in this area in the past were the Maurya, members of a large empire which had dominated this part of India from around 300 BCE to 180 BCE. However, these bricks and other artifacts which included finely carved pieces of soapstone were clearly much older than this.

The only known older Indian civilization was one formed by Aryan settlers, nomadic cattle-herders who arrived via the Kush Mountains from Persia and central Asia around 1200 BCE, but these people had established their towns and cities in the Ganges Valley, far from the Punjab. For many years, the bricks and other remains found in the Punjab remained a mystery largely ignored by historians and archaeologists. A British amateur archaeologist and army engineer, Sir Alexander Cunningham, visited the site of the railway construction near Harappa and discovered what appeared to be a carved seal buried near the track bed. He published a monograph on this find in 1872, though he mistakenly attributed this to around 400 BCE.

In 1912, another British amateur archaeologist, John Faithfull Fleet, a senior member of the Indian Civil Service, visited the site at Harappa and discovered more odd seals. He recognized that these were much older than had previously been thought and, for the first time, archaeologists began to wonder whether the bricks discovered at Harappa provided evidence of an unknown Indian civilization.

In 1921, the director-general of the Archaeological Survey of India, Sir John Hubert Marshall, organized an expedition to undertake a major dig at Harappa and appointed one of his assistants, Indian archaeologist Daya Ram Sahni, to supervise. The dig continued into the following year and what was discovered was truly astounding; the site on the banks of the Ravi River was the remains of an enormous city which seemed to have thrived from around 2500 BCE to 1900 BCE. This wasn't just a very large and previously undiscovered city; it was evidence of a much older civilization in the area than anyone had ever suspected.

The city became known as Harappa, the name of the nearby village which was constructed on top of parts of the ruins, and the civilization which it belonged to was named the Harappan Civilization because it seemed that this must have been a major or perhaps the capital city of these people. During the next ten years, a series of excavations at Harappa and at another site called Mohenjo-daro on the banks of the Indus River near the town of Larkana uncovered many more ruins. By 1931, it was clear that the ancient history of India was much more complex and stretched back much further than anyone had previously realized.

Chapter Two

Excavation of Harappa

"Archaeology holds all the keys to understanding who we are and where we come from."

—Sarah Parcak

Merely one hundred years ago, no-one even suspected the existence of a large, ancient, complex, and sophisticated civilization in the Indus River Valley. The archaeology which began in earnest in the 1920s at Harappa has led to a developing understanding of this culture which is changing even today. Unlike other contemporary civilizations which have been known almost since the time that they declined (the Ancient Egyptian, for example), archaeologists and anthropologists are still trying to piece together a picture of what the Indus Valley Civilization may have looked like, how far it stretched, and what happened to it. What we can now be certain of is that the Indus Valley Civilization (which is sometimes still referred to as the Harappan Civilization) was one of the earliest complex, urban human civilizations.

It should be noted that this ancient civilization is also sometimes called the Sarasvati Civilization or the Indus-Sarasvati Civilization as it has been identified by some people as the Vedic civilization which was said to have existed by the mythical Sarasvati River in traditional Hindu teachings. Archaeologists have discovered that there may have been another river in this area in ancient times, running parallel and to the east of the Indus and some consider that this may have been the fabled Sarasvati.

Since the discovery of the lost city of Harappa in the 1920s, there have been many subsequent archaeological expeditions in this area which have added to our understanding of this civilization. Initially, much of this work was done under the auspices of the British-controlled Archaeological Survey of India. When Britain relinquished control of India in 1947, it led to the creation of two separate and autonomous countries: The Republic of India and the Islamic Republic of Pakistan. Many of the sites initially associated with the Indus Valley Civilization were in the portion of the Punjab which became part of Pakistan. However, subsequent discoveries have revealed that the area controlled by the Harappans was much larger than previously understood and new sites have been discovered, not just in other parts of Pakistan and India but as far north as present-day Afghanistan. To the present day, more than 1,000 archaeological sites which appear to have belonged to this society have been uncovered, and more are being discovered almost every year.

It is now generally accepted that the Indus Valley was one of the three Ancient east societies considered to be the cradles of civilization. However, the other two (Egypt and Mesopotamia) left written records which means we know a great deal about those people. The Indus people left few written records, and the inscriptions which have been found on seals and other artifacts have not yet been deciphered. This means that we know comparatively little about this civilization despite the fact that it may have been the largest of all.

Although there is still dispute about precisely when Indus Valley Civilization rose to prominence, most historians now describe the development of these people in three distinct periods: The Early Harappan Phase (3300 to 2600 BCE), the Mature Harappan Phase (2600 to 1900 BCE), and the Late Harappan Phase (1900 to 1300 BCE).

Another reason that this important civilization is not remembered in the same way as, for example, the Egyptian and Mesopotamian civilizations was that these people did not build massive, monumental structures. There were no pyramids and no ziggurats or enormous tombs which survived the demise of the cultures which built them. These people did not bury great wealth with their dead, which meant that their ancient sites were not of interest to those who sought treasure. After its decline, little was left of the Indus Valley Civilization other than piles of old bricks buried in the dusty earth of the Punjab and a vague memory that this had once been the location of a mighty city. As their buildings and cities fell into ruin, these people were largely forgotten.

The Indus people also do not seem to have been as warlike as most other ancient civilizations. They do not seem to have attempted to conquer other cultures, and few indications of warfare or weapons have been discovered in archaeological excavations of Indus Valley Civilization sites.

It seems that the Harappans were a peaceful people who lived in sizeable communities without large-scale conflict and who felt no need to create monumental buildings or tombs or to inter their dead with their wealth. As the history of these people was gradually uncovered during the twentieth century, these differences made them particularly fascinating to historians and anthropologists. Just why did this culture develop in the way that it did and what happened to cause it to suddenly disappear?

However, our understanding of the Indus Valley Civilization is still evolving. As recently as 2016, an archaeological expedition organized by the Archaeological Survey of India (ASI) published a report which suggested that the beginning of the Indus Valley Civilization may have happened much earlier than is generally accepted. The leader of this project, Anindya Sarkar, noted that he believed that it is possible that this culture originated as early as 6000 BCE. This would make this the oldest of all the ancient civilizations. Sarkar's theory is still being debated by historians and anthropologists.

It seems likely that continuing excavations and new discoveries may continue to change what we know about the Indus Valley Civilization in the future.

Chapter Three

Origins

"Every civilization emerges out of interactions with others, but nevertheless creates its own miracle."

—Romila Thapar

The first people known to have lived in the Indus River Valley were bands of nomadic hunter-gatherers who appeared around 10000 BCE in what is known as the Foraging Era. These people lived in small groups and their settlements comprised temporary, portable homes. They followed game and picked whatever wild fruits, berries, and roots they could find.

Around 7000 BCE, some of these people began to use simple tools to build permanent settlements and to practice agriculture. They ceased to be nomadic and became sedentary. This era has become known as the Early Food Producing Era, and this process happened in other parts of the world at around the same time. It wasn't a single, sudden change of lifestyle but a gradual evolution as people began to devise more efficient ways of producing food. Both nomadic and sedentary groups co-existed with each other with some people living in small settlements and farming while others continued to live an essentially Stone Age lifestyle.

One of the first centers of human settlement in the Indus Valley has been discovered in Mehrgarh on the Kacchi Plain in Baluchistan, the southwestern region of present-day Pakistan. The beginning of this settlement has been traced to around 7000 BCE, and there is evidence of farming of wheat and barley as well as ash mounds and other items which suggest that the people who lived here also herded cattle, goats, and sheep. By 5000 BCE, there is evidence that the people who lived here were trading with other cultures as far away as the coast of the Arabian Sea and central Asia.

Mehrgarh was just one of several centers which gradually developed in this region during the Early Food Producing Era, and by the beginning of the Regionalization Era in 5500 BCE, many had developed trade and trade routes with other cultures. By this time, some of the small settlements had grown into towns and, though these were primitive people, archaeologists have discovered surprising evidence that they were more advanced than expected in some ways. For example, some human remains discovered at Mehrgarh show signs that these people practiced a form of dentistry. Several sets of remains show evidence that their teeth were drilled while they were alive, something that didn't happen in other parts of the world until much later.

However, in general we do not know much about the people who developed the Indus Valley. It is believed that this culture emerged from early settlements such as Mehrgarh rather than from outsiders, but the complete lack of written records makes this no more than an educated guess.

Chapter Four

Early Harappan Phase: 3300 to 2600 BCE

"The diversity of India, of our civilization, is actually a thing of beauty, which is something we are extremely proud of."

—Narendra Modi

By around 3500 BCE, some settlements in the Indus Valley had developed pottery and more sophisticated tools and had become what historians call settled agro-pastoral communities. In an area close to the Ravi River, the first settlements associated with the Indus Valley Civilization were formed (this part of the Early Harappan Phase is sometimes called the Ravi Phase) including the first establishment of a settlement at Harappa.

It is believed that Harappa in particular began to grow because it was located on an important junction of several trade routes linking the Upper Indus Valley with the southern plains. Another large settlement, Jalilpur, is around 72 kilometers to the southwest of Harappa while Rajanpur is on the opposite bank of the Ravi, around 77 kilometers to the northeast. The idea that this was a trade center has been reinforced because excavations on the site of Harappa have uncovered many artifacts which came from other areas. For example, grinding stones found in Harappa are known to have originated in the Kirana Hills, north of Rajanpur, and other items are made of grey chert and steatite which come from mountains in the north as far away as present-day Afghanistan and from the Sulaiman Mountains in the west.

In its earliest stages, wheel-thrown pottery was being produced in Harappa, and the buildings were being made from mud bricks produced to a very consistent size ratio of 1:2:4. This fixed ratio for bricks was continued throughout the history of the Indus Valley Civilization, and almost all buildings were constructed of mud bricks bound with mortar—there was very little use of worked or carved stone.

Other crafts also proliferated in the earliest stages of Harappa. Archaeologists have discovered terracotta figurines of animals and humans and even children's toys. Although no examples have been found, it is also believed that there was textile production in Harappa at this time, evidenced by the impression of cloth left in clay items as well as the finding of spindle whorls and weaving tools associated with textile production.

All these things suggest that this was a complex, multi-layered society with artisans who were not part of the food production process. This, in turn, suggests some form of central control as well as agriculture which was sufficiently efficient to feed large numbers of people.

The precise number of people who lived in Harappa in its earliest stages is not precisely known, though the city at this time was spread over more than ten hectares with what appear to be two smaller settlements to the immediate north and south. By 2800 BCE, Harappa had expanded greatly, and during this period (usually identified as the Kot Diji Phase) the city covered 25 hectares and parts of the city were protected by massive mud-brick walls incorporating large gateways.

Although the construction method during this phase also used mud bricks, these were generally constructed using molds rather than the earlier hand-made bricks. The same proportions were retained, but smaller bricks were used for houses and other domestic buildings while a larger size was used for city walls. The architecture of the city also became much more complex during this period. Most buildings within the city were constructed on brick platforms which lifted them above the earth below. The city included an intricate and well-designed sanitation and drainage system which was much more sophisticated than anything found in contemporary cities in Mesopotamia or Egypt (and considerably more effective than the sanitation systems in some present-day towns in India and Pakistan). Many houses had their own wells and those that didn't had access to a community well providing clean water. Additionally, many homes had baths and flush toilets which drained into the sewage system below. Underground drains led to large brick soil tanks and clay pots which acted as septic tanks. These were fitted with manhole covers to allow for periodic cleaning. Such complex and sophisticated sanitation and waste disposal has not been found in any other ancient culture and would not become widespread in Europe until more than 4,000 years later.

Different areas of Harappa were dedicated to different things, with residential areas, areas where artisans produced goods, and areas dedicated to trading. The city was surrounded by a large number of smaller settlements on the banks of the Indus River and scattered across the Punjab plain. In addition to trading links to other areas and cultures, it also seems certain that there were links between Harappa and at least one of the other major cities of the Indus Valley Civilization, Mohenjo-daro, around 640 kilometers (400 miles) away.

The construction of the main part of Mohenjo-daro began around 2600 BCE, and this city, located west of the Indus River in the province of Sindh, grew to become the largest of all the Indus River Valley Civilization cities. Mohenjo-daro did not grow in the haphazard way in which most cities of this period did—it was obviously the result of careful planning with a grid of streets laid out at right angles and clear demarcation between the different districts of the city. There were also large granaries and even structures which are thought to have been public bath-houses. Mohenjo-daro also featured a central citadel, an area protected by thick walls at the center of the city which presumably housed high-status families and the administration which ran the city.

Virtually every house so far excavated in Mohenjo-daro had not only a flush toilet but also a bath, generally mounted on a brick platform. The smaller houses so far discovered had two rooms, and the largest was very large indeed, covering 800 square meters (8,600 square feet, around four times the size of the average house in the United States today). Streets were aligned on a north-south grid and were to a standardized design—main streets were 9 meters (29 feet) wide, less important streets were around 3 meters (10 feet) wide, and alleys were 1.5 meters (5 feet). This basic design, with a north-south grid and uniform width streets was repeated in virtually every Indus Valley urban center including even relatively small settlements.

There are however some notable things that have not been discovered at Harappa, Mohenjo-daro, or any other Indus city. Archaeologists have not discovered any buildings which have been identified as royal palaces, temples, or military centers. This has led to speculation about just how this culture was organized and administered. Town planning and the obvious complexity of these cities make it certain that this was a sophisticated society with some form of centralized control. However, the lack of palaces has led scholars to speculate that this was not a culture which was ruled by a monarchical elite as were, for example, the Mesopotamian and Egyptian civilizations.

Instead, the multiple walled sectors of Indus Valley Civilization cities suggest that this culture was ruled by some form of corporate group or groups, perhaps comprising landowners, merchants, or ritual specialists. It is possible that such groups, possibly divided into families, may have governed cities relatively independently, so that Harappa and Mohenjo-daro may have been some of the earliest examples of city-states, with the cities themselves and the surrounding lands ruled by a small group. Each city-state would have been independent, but there was also clearly cooperation and trade between the cities. There is also no evidence of conflict between individual cities as there was, for example, amongst the city-states of Mesopotamia which again suggests some form of overarching co-operation.

The cities of the Indus Valley Civilization were virtually unique amongst ancient cities, not just because they were carefully planned and took account of the need for sanitation, but because they seem to have lacked large temples and palaces and to have lived at peace with each other, with no evidence that one city attempted to impose control over the others. That makes this culture very unusual but, unfortunately, the lack of written records means that we can only guess the form that their society took.

Chapter Five

Life and Death in the Indus Valley

"The greatest advances of civilization, whether in architecture or painting, in science and literature, in industry or agriculture, have never come from centralized government."

—Milton Friedman

The excavation of a single cemetery at the archaeological site at Harappa gives some indication of how the people of the Indus Valley treated their dead. However, the remains of only around 200 people have been found, and these people were buried over a period of 700 years (from around 2600 BCE to 1900 BCE). Clearly, this represents only a tiny fraction of the people who lived and died in the city during this extended period, which suggests that the vast bulk of people were treated differently after death, perhaps being cremated.

There is a great deal of consistency in the remains discovered to date. Almost all the females were buried with shell bangles on their left arm. Later burials contain very finely made and fragile bangles, which may suggest that these women were not required to undertake manual labor. Some female burials included a small bronze mirror and several were wearing small black or green pendants around their necks.

Most male burials do not seem to have included jewelry or personal items, though one male burial included a very elaborate headdress made from thousands of tiny steatite beads and a few included small gold beads. Both male and female burials included small pottery vessels, which may originally have contained food offerings, though this is not certain. These burial practices are notably different to those of other contemporary ancient civilizations where the dead were often interred with high-value items including jewelry and weapons denoting the status of the dead person.

Analysis of the remains by physical anthropologists suggests that many of these women buried in Harappa were related, indicating that these burials may be those of a particular family or clan. Other analysis shows that while some of these people were born and raised in or around Harappa, others came from outside areas. The other thing that is notable about these remains is that they are generally fairly healthy. There are some indications of abscesses and arthritis and some evidence that the dead may have suffered from very high fevers, such as those associated with malaria, but in general, these remains show few indications of congenital defects or long-term debilitating conditions, and none of the dead seem to have died as the result of trauma.

This, combined with a complete lack of discoveries of shields or armor or other items associated with warfare, suggests that these were not a particularly warlike people. Items like bronze spears and swords as well as arrowheads have been found, but it is presumed that most of these were produced for hunting or for personal self-defense rather than for use by large-scale military organizations. No-one has discovered any evidence of any large-scale battle or war during the period of this civilization.

Other discoveries at Harappa and other sites include large numbers of seals of various kinds. Some of these seals are molded in terracotta while others are carved from steatite, a hard metamorphic rock. Many of the seals incorporate animal designs of elephants, tigers, water buffaloes, and other animals as well as what appears to be some form of script. However, to date, all attempts to decipher this script (which also appears on amulets, pottery, and other artifacts) have failed. The seals, one of the most commonly recovered items in Harappa and Mohenjo-daro, appear to have been used for the identification of property as well as for stamping in wet clay on trade goods.

One recent discovery is that some seals discovered at Akkadian sites in Mesopotamia originate from the Indus Valley. Many of these incorporate Akkadian text in addition to the original script. It is hoped that the Akkadian writing (which has been deciphered) is a direct translation of the original script on the seals; this may help historians understand the writing of the Indus Valley Civilization.

Another aspect of the daily life of this culture which has emerged following archaeological excavation is that the Indus people were amongst the first to develop a standardized system of weights and measures. An ivory measuring scale discovered at a Harappan site had divisions which were 1.7 millimeters (0.07 inches) in length, the smallest measurement of length found in any Bronze Age culture. Weights were similarly carefully measured using standardized hexahedron chert weights.

Other artifacts recovered from archaeological sites suggest that this culture developed advanced metal-working skills. Items made from bronze, copper lead, and tin have been discovered. Several finely carved items made from the semi-precious gemstone carnelian have been found at Harappa and Mohenjo-daro. Other items made from seashells have also been discovered, and some of these originate from as far away as the coast of Oman, confirming that the Indus Valley Civilization traded widely and with a number of other cultures.

Other items recovered at Harappa are made from minerals from Iran and Afghanistan, lead and copper from different parts of India, and jade from China. Some items are constructed from cedar wood from the Himalayas and Kashmir, which was most likely transported by being floated down rivers. The people of the Indus Valley Civilization appear to have been confident seafarers who built small boats and larger ships with which they traded with other civilizations.

Excavations at the coastal city of Lothal have revealed what appears to be a large dock, and it is believed that people from the Indus Valley sailed ships made from planks of cedar wood and equipped with large sails made from cloth or woven rushes on the Red Sea, the Arabian Gulf, and the Persian Gulf. This allowed contacts with other cultures in Mesopotamia and perhaps also with Egypt and as far as Crete. Ancient Akkadian texts refer to a culture called Meluhha with which they traded around 2500 BCE to 2000 BCE. It is thought that Meluhha refers to the Indus Valley Civilization, which seems likely considering the large number of Indus artifacts that have been found at ancient sites in Mesopotamia.

However, trading wasn't only conducted by sea. The Indus Valley Civilization also traded widely with other parts of present-day India and as far north as present-day Afghanistan. The Harappans were thought to have been amongst the first of the ancient people to use wheeled vehicles, and the ox carts they used were not very different to the carts which can still be seen in some parts of India and Pakistan.

In terms of religion, we know relatively little about the people of the Indus Valley Civilization. None of the excavations undertaken so far have uncovered any large temples or religious centers. The prevalence of animal symbology on seals, amulets, and pottery has led some historians to speculate that these people may have been involved in some type of animal cult. Some of the imagery seems to support this as it shows part-human, part-animal creatures—for example, one seal shows a creature which has the trunk of an elephant, the hindquarters of a tiger, the hind legs of a bull, and the face of a human. There are also many symbols which appear to show unicorns—

something that was almost unique to this culture and which virtually disappeared when it ended.

These people may also have been involved in fertility cults as many recovered artifacts are phallic or show pregnant females. Some carved tablets appear to show large processions, which may have had some religious significance. Some sculptures show men with their hair tied back in a particular way, and some historians have wondered whether these could be priests of some sort.

Historians have also wondered whether water played a part in the religious rituals of these people. The prevalence of baths in houses may suggest this, and some larger structures have been discovered which appear to have been public baths. The Great Bath at Mohenjo-daro, for example, is around 12 meters (39 feet) long, 7 meters (23 feet) wide, and 2.5 meters (8 feet) deep, about the size of a modern swimming pool. It has steps leading to the bottom and is constructed of bricks sealed with bitumen. The bottom slopes towards a single drain. The Great Bath may have been the site of ritual bathing, similar to the rituals which take place on the Ganges River today.

Unlike the contemporary civilizations in Egypt and Mesopotamia, there is no evidence that Indus Valley Civilization relied on the use of slave labor. It appears that wealth was generated by craftsmen, artisans, and merchants. A standardized system of weights and measures ensured that trade was fair and may also have been used to levy taxes.

It seems that the Indus people also enjoyed games. Game boards which resemble modern chess boards and maze-like games which involved the maneuvering of small balls have been found. Dice games were also probably played—at Mohenjo-daro a die has been found which is marked identically to the modern, six-faced die.

We don't know a great deal about how the people of the Indus Valley Civilization looked or dressed, and what little information we have comes mainly from figurines and statues. It seems that the women of this culture wore a short skirt made of cotton or wool and generally wore their hair in a bun, in braids, in locks, or tucked into some form of turban. Some make-up and toiletry items and special combs have also been recovered from Harappan sites, and some terracotta figures of women seem to have had their hair colored red, suggesting that this may also have been done by women. Many Harappan males seem to have worn beards, and they are generally depicted as bareheaded though some are shown wearing turbans.

Chapter Six

Mature Harappan Phase: 2600 to 1900 BCE

"India has an enthralling, uplifting civilization that sparkles not only in our magnificent art, but also in the enormous creativity and humanity of our daily life in city and village."

—Pranab Mukherjee

The regular monsoons which flooded the Indus River and its tributaries ensured that farmland remained fertile, allowing the production of large agricultural surpluses. The resulting increase in population led to more and larger cities. By 2600 BCE, the Indus Valley Civilization included at least six major urban centers in addition to Harappa and Mohenjo-daro. These were Ganeriwala in present-day Pakistan and Dholavira, Kalibangan, Rakhigarhi, Rupar, and the coastal city of Lothal, all in present-day India. Over 1,000 archaeological sites attributed to this civilization have been identified, mostly close to the Indus River. At its peak, the Indus Valley Civilization is estimated to have included an astounding five million people and was larger than Ancient Egypt and Mesopotamia combined.

Although the cities grew, the egalitarianism seen in the early phase of Harappan Civilization continued. Although some houses were bigger than others, there were no palaces and every house had access to clean water and efficient waste disposal. Anthropologists use the term "wealth concentration" to describe the way in which the wealth of a society is distributed. In many ancient civilizations, the bulk of wealth was held by rulers or a ruling elite while the majority of people lived in relative poverty. In the case of the Indus Valley Civilization, this does not appear to have been true—this was a society with a very low wealth concentration.

During this period, the urbanization of the Indus Valley Civilization increased. Harappa and Mohenjo-daro remained large and significant urban centers, but they were surpassed in size by other, growing cities. The largest of all was Rakhigarhi in the Hisar district in present-day India. The site covers almost 350 hectares (by comparison, Harappa covered around 150 hectares in the same period), and it may have been occupied by a population of up to 50,000 people. Like the other Indus Valley cities, Rakhigarhi featured a central, walled citadel built on top of a mound and surrounded by large residential, trade, and artisan districts.

Another large city has been found at Lurewala in the central Indus Valley. This site covered 200 hectares and was thought to have been occupied at its height by more than 35,000 people. A slightly smaller site was discovered at Dholavira in the state of Gujarat in western India. This site covered around 100 hectares and had some distinct features. The city was built in an area of desert climate and where it may rain only once every four or five years. Dholavira incorporated one of the first water conservation systems discovered anywhere in the ancient world. The people who lived in this city created 16 or more massive stone reservoirs which were used to store rainwater. The city also featured massive walls constructed using sandstone blocks faced with a veneer of finished stone, something which has not been seen in any other Indus site. Excavations at Dholavira have also revealed a large stadium building, which may have been used for religious purposes.

One other interesting find at Dholavira was what appears to be a massive signboard which was discovered in a room off one of the main gates to the city. This was originally a large wooden board, almost three meters long, on which ten symbols made out of pieces of gypsum were arranged. The board fell to the ground at some point, and the wood rotted, but the pieces of gypsum remained in place and were discovered by archaeologists. This was clearly some sort of public signboard but, unfortunately, the Harappan script has not been deciphered, so we have no idea what it meant. Around 400 different symbols have been found in the Indus script, and these are thought to be logo-syllabic (each symbol representing a single word), but until some bilingual artifacts are found which include writing in deciphered texts, it will be difficult to be certain of the meaning of these symbols.

Many scholars believe that there is a relationship between the Harappan script and the Dravidian languages spoken by more than 200 million people in present-day India, Pakistan, and Sri Lanka. The earliest examples of the written form of these languages have been dated at 200 BCE, and these may in part derive from the earlier language of the Indus Valley Civilization. For this reason, some historians refer to the language of the Indus Valley Civilization as proto-Dravidian.

It is notable that even the smaller towns and settlements of this period show evidence of careful planning. Where most settlements of the ancient world began as small villages and grew in a haphazard way to become towns or cities, that is clearly not the case here. Even small settlements are laid out in a logical grid pattern. This uniformity of design and planning across virtually every Indus site suggests that there was some form of over-riding state control or, at the very least, close co-operation between a large number of city-states.

During this period, the agriculture practiced by these people developed and expanded. Wheat, barley, sesame, rice, and millet were grown at Harappa and other sites. Harappa and other sites also show evidence of the cultivation of a number of other crops including grapes, cotton, peas, gram, chickpea, and garlic. Plows were used, as evidenced by the discovery of terracotta miniature plows. Domestic animals included oxen, cattle, sheep, and goats as well as dogs which were presumably used for herding and as guards. In addition to domestic animals, excavations suggest that these people also ate more exotic animals including rhinoceros, monkey, peacock, and camel.

Trade continued to be an important part of life in the Indus Valley Civilization in this period. Imports included fish, raw wool, and silver from Mesopotamia, lapis lazuli from Afghanistan, tin from Kazakhstan, and chlorite and greenschist from the Persian Gulf. Exports included items made from gold, carnelian, ebony, ivory, and tortoiseshell as well as animals including monkeys and birds.

The burials discovered at other Indus Valley Civilization sites were similar to those discovered at Harappa. Most were relatively simple—bodies were placed in pits or brick chambers, usually placed so that the head faced north. Items were sometimes interred with the bodies; these were usually food, pottery, and perhaps ornaments, but nothing of high value. There is also evidence of urn burials, suggesting that cremated remains were interred in this way.

During the Mature Harappan Phase, the Indus Valley Civilization reached its greatest extent. It may have included up to 5 million people spread over 1.5 million square kilometers (600,000 square miles). The lands controlled by this civilization stretched from Shortugai on the Oxus River in Afghanistan in the north to Daimabad on the Pravara River in Maharashtra in India in the south, and from Sutkagen-dor on the Pakistan-Iran border in the west to Alamgirpur on the Yamuna River in Uttar Pradesh in India in the east.

This is a huge area, and yet it seems that the Indus people occupied these lands without major battles or wars of conquest. In contrast to other ancient cultures, the people of this civilization seem to have lived peacefully and with better sanitation and public health than any contemporary civilization. They seem to have done this by becoming experts at agriculture and animal husbandry and by developing extensive trade networks both within the Indus Valley, with other parts of India, and with distant cultures.

The uniformity of planning in the cities of this civilization added to what appears to be public amenities such as roads and baths which could only have been created using some form of taxation, making it likely that there was some form of overarching government, though there is no evidence that this culture was ruled by a single leader or king. The people who lived in this area after the disappearance of the Indus Valley Civilization, the Aryan tribes, were organized into small family and tribal groups, each ruled by a local chief, a *Rajah*. Rajahs ruled with the help and advice of a council of elders of the tribe and, though each tribe was separate and independent, there was co-operation between tribes. Some anthropologists have speculated that this model of governance was copied from what existed under the Indus Valley Civilization, with each city-state being ruled by a leader or a council of high-status people and with some form of high-level council being responsible for co-operation and planning between city-states.

Chapter Seven

Late Harappan Phase: 1900 to 1300 BCE

"We have indeed, come upon a striking example of the decay of an once honorable city, the cause of which we suspect to be the vagaries of the Indus rather than pressure by invaders."

—Ernest Mackay

At the beginning of this phase, the Indus Valley Civilization was at its most powerful and had reached its greatest extent. However, from around 1800 BCE, the culture began a slow decline. The possible reasons for this will be discussed in the next chapter, but some Indus cities began to slowly lose population until, by the end of this phase, they were virtually abandoned. Other sites seem to have suffered a more abrupt change, seemingly becoming uninhabited and abandoned in a very short period.

This was not only a period of de-urbanization; it was also a time when the use of some of the major Indus cities changed. For example, in Mohenjo-daro excavations have showed that the central part of the city, sometimes called the citadel, which appears to have previously been occupied by high-status residences, was turned over to use by artisans, particularly potters. This strongly suggests a significant change in the social order of the city. In his book *Indus Civilization* (1935), archaeologist Ernest Mackay notes: "This quarter of Manhenjodro, if not the whole of city, must by this time have declined greatly in social standing and organization, for it is difficult to imagine that the city authorities . . . would have allowed potters to practice their craft within the confines of the city."

Other excavations have revealed that even the quality of construction began to decline during this period—the masonry created during this period was notably less impressive than the construction work undertaken during the Mature Harappan Phase. Town planning also seems to have virtually disappeared during this phase—the few new settlements created during the Late Harappan Phase lacked the grid layout which characterized earlier settlements. Even the complex and sophisticated drainage and sanitation systems which were found in almost every earlier Harappan settlement were either absent completely or less well designed—many houses still had access to drains, but excavation reveals that these were of much simpler design and they do not seem to have been maintained to the same high standard.

Some towns and cities vanished altogether in this period. In the Mature Harappan Phase, there were 175 settlements in the Bahawalpur region, close to the Hakra River. By the middle of the Late Harappan Phase, there were just 50. Other cities were reduced in size.

Many of the new settlements which were established during this period were in the east of the region controlled by the Indus Valley Civilization, in the Ganga-Yamuna plains. There seems to have been a general movement away from large urban centers and towards smaller, rural communities and many of these are to the east, suggesting a general move of the population in this direction.

Even the ceramics produced changed during this period. During the Mature Harappan Phase a great deal of pottery was produced which featured a distinctive style, with bold, black designs on a red background. This style persisted for many hundreds of years but, during the late Harappan Phase, it suddenly ceased to be produced and instead plainer, buff-colored pottery was created which was of reduced quality and featured a smaller range of simpler designs. The seals which have been found in large quantities during excavations of earlier phases of this society also seem to have stopped being made—virtually no seals have been found at Late Harappan Phase sites.

Luxury items such as sculptures, jewelry, terracotta figures, and the elaborate inlaid ivory work found at earlier sites are also absent in sites from the late period. Excavations have revealed that during this period people living in cities began for the first time hiding their valuables under the floors of their homes. This had not been seen before, and it suggests a breakdown of the social order leading people to fear robbery or burglary, something which they had not done before. Some excavations have found what appear to be unburied bodies in cities, suggesting that these people were simply left where they died. This was not seen in excavations of earlier periods.

Taking all these things together, it is clear that something fundamental happened to the Indus Valley Civilization, starting in approximately 1800 BCE. The urbanization and careful planning of towns and cities which had gone before declined. The advanced building techniques seemed to be forgotten, and even the sanitation and waste disposal which had been such an integral part of every previous city was abandoned.

The decline of the Indus Valley Civilization was not progressive or according to a fixed pattern. Some sites seem to have been abandoned and then re-occupied anything up to 100 years later. What does seem to be certain is that in the Late Harappan Phase there was a general move of the population of the Indus Valley Civilization to the south and east.

By 1700 BCE, several major Indus cities appear to have been completely abandoned. Even in cities such as Mohenjo-daro there was a notable decline—during this period, for example, the great bath was built over and fell into disuse. The farmers continued to work their fields, but the cities declined sharply until, by 1300 BCE, all the cities of this once mighty culture were abandoned and in ruins, leaving behind only piles of bricks in the dusty earth.

The question that has provided a great deal of debate and disagreement amongst historians is: just what happened to cause the complete disappearance of the Indus Valley Civilization?

Chapter Eight

Downfall of the Indus Valley Civilization

"A great civilization is not conquered from without until it has destroyed itself from within."

—Ariel Durant

There is no agreement amongst historians as to what led to the end of the Indus Valley Civilization. There are four main theories as to what may have happened: climate change, a sudden cessation of outside trade links, a change in the course of the Indus River, or an invasion. Let's look at these in turn.

Climate change. During the course of the Indus Valley Civilization, there is some evidence that the region close to the Indus River became increasingly arid. The main reason seems to have been a shift in the area in which the monsoon rains occurred. As this culture grew, there is evidence that the monsoon gradually increased and moved to the east. The regular inundation caused by the monsoon kept the arable land close to the major cities fertile without the need to build complex irrigation systems. However, if the monsoon continued to move to the east, the land close to the Indus River would have become less productive and would have been unable to produce the food surpluses needed to support the populations of large urban centers.

Historians who accept this cause for the decline of the Indus Valley Civilization suggest that this explains why large segments of the population seemed to migrate towards the east and the Ganges Basin. However, the new farming land was not as fertile as the land close to the Indus River had been and did not produce the food surpluses needed to support the workforce required for the construction of new cities or continuing trade with other cultures. In that sense, climate change in the form of gradual aridification could well account for the gradual decline of the Indus Valley Civilization and might also explain why the population seems to have migrated to the east.

However, it should be noted that other historians have suggested that the decline of the Indus Valley Civilization was caused not by a general lack of water, but by extreme flooding events. Evidence of large-scale flooding has been found at Mohenjo-daro, Kalibangan, and Dholavira. In each case, archaeologists have found collapsed buildings and streets covered in silt clay which have subsequently been built on. In Mohenjo-daro it is believed that this serious flooding happened at least three times. The city of Chanhudaro also appears to have been completely destroyed by large inundations on at least two occasions. Even in 2010, flooding continued to be a problem in this area—in that year the Harappan archaeological site at Jognakhera was submerged under more than ten feet of water when the Sutlej Yamuna link canal overflowed following heavy rain.

Flooding on this scale would also have impacted agriculture, perhaps causing food shortages and forcing people to move away from these areas. There is no agreement amongst historians on what could have caused this periodic and massive flooding, though some have suggested tectonic events may have created a temporary natural dam to stop the flow of the Indus River before this was somehow released to cause flooding downstream.

Cessation of trade. Around 2200 BCE, climatic change had a devastating effect on the Akkadian Empire in Mesopotamia. Excavations at the Akkadian city of Shekhna, for example, showed not only that the city was abandoned around this time, but that all signs of life in the earth itself including earthworms vanished for almost 300 years. Research suggests that this was associated with something called the "4.2-kiloyear BP aridification event," which was caused by a drop in the surface temperature of the North Atlantic and which led to disruption in the flow and regular flooding of the Tigris and Euphrates Rivers.

However, the effects of this event were felt well beyond Mesopotamia. The River Nile was also affected and the Old Kingdom of Egypt which had lasted for more than 500 years was suddenly destroyed by a wave of famines and subsequent social breakdown. Even on the Arabian Peninsula, the Umm al-Nar Culture which had been in existence for hundreds of years suddenly vanished. Mesopotamia, Pharaonic Egypt, and the Arabian Peninsula had all been major trading partners for the

Indus Valley Civilization, and suddenly all three were no longer a viable destination for exports or a source of imports.

There has been speculation that this culture had become reliant on both imports and exports to such an extent that the sudden removal of most trading partners led to social disintegration and the eventual abandonment of major cities.

Change in the course of the Indus River. Geological surveys have shown that the Indus River has changed its course dramatically and on several occasions. This may have been due to silt build-up causing the creation of natural dams and deflecting the flow of the river, or perhaps it could have been caused by tectonic events—the Indus River Valley is seismically active.

During the period from 8000 to 4000 BCE, the Indus River had two separate courses, with the Jacobabad course on the western edge of the valley and the Nara River running parallel on the eastern edge of the plains. During the period from 4000 to 2000 BCE, the two rivers gradually shifted to the east. Mohenjo-daro was originally located between the two rivers, and as they changed course this may have led to the abandonment of this city. In the upper reaches of the Indus, smaller rivers such as the Ravi and the Beas also changed course several times, and there is archaeological evidence that Indus settlements were occupied and then abandoned as the rivers moved.

It certainly seems possible that changes in the course of rivers on which the agriculture of the Indus Valley

Civilization was so reliant may have had a devastating effect on individual settlements and even cities, but many historians doubt that this could account for the complete destruction of a culture which was so widespread and so diverse.

Invasion. When historians first became aware of the existence of the Indus Valley Civilization in the 1920s, there was a widespread assumption that the destruction of this culture was caused by an invasion from outside the region. One of the first academic books about this civilization, *The Indus Civilization*, was written in 1953 by British historian and archaeologist Sir Mortimer Wheeler. The book postulated that the culture was destroyed following an invasion by Aryan migrants from central Asia who arrived with well-organized armies and advanced weapons and swept the largely agrarian and peaceful Harappans aside.

The evidence for this included the discovery of numbers of unburied bodies in some Indus Valley Civilization cities including Harappa and Mohenjo-daro. Wheeler combined this with a reading of the Rigveda, an ancient Indian Vedic Sanskrit text which forms one of the four Vedas of Hinduism. These texts mention a war between incoming Aryans and the indigenous people of the Indus Valley and even includes details of the Aryan conquest of "Hariyupia" which Wheeler took to be a record of the sack of Harappa. For many years, this was accepted as being the most likely cause of the end of the Indus Valley Civilization, but more recent re-assessment of the evidence has thrown this conclusion into doubt.

For example, it has noted that none of the apparently unburied bodies found in Indus Valley Civilization cities shown evidence of the sort of trauma that would be associated with a massacre or death in battle. It has also been noted that the Harappan culture had completely disappeared by 1300 BCE, whereas the Rigveda was not written until 300 years later, around 1000 BCE. So, the Rigveda cannot be taken as a contemporary account; it is rather a historical account directed by oral tradition, religious belief, and myth.

Finally, many anthropologists have noted that, if the Indus Valley Civilization had been conquered by another culture from the outside, there would have been an inevitable melding of arts, crafts, and social structure which should be immediately apparent in recovered artifacts. However, nothing of this sort has been discovered. The production of ceramics and other craft items continued up to the final disappearance of the Harappan culture but, while items produced during the Late Harappan Phase are simpler and cruder than those produced during the Mature Harappan Phase, they do not show any signs of being influenced by a foreign invasion. For these reasons, the theory that the Indus Valley Civilization was destroyed by an invasion is now largely discredited.

Instead, many historians have come to the conclusion that there was no single cause for the decline of the Indus Valley Civilization. Instead, they believe that a combination of factors, which include environmental changes combined with declining trade, led to a process of de-urbanization. According to this school of thought, the Indus Valley Civilization did not end at all; it simply devolved into smaller settlements which covered a similar area, but which no longer produced the kind of agricultural surpluses required to support a complex bureaucracy, an artisan class, or the creation and maintenance of large cities.

This theory suggests that what has been called the emergence of post-Harappan cultures in the Indus Valley should actually be regarded as a post-urban phase of the Harappan culture. According to this view, the Indus Valley Civilization did not disappear after 1300 BCE, but rather the integrated social, political, and economic system which had allowed the construction of mighty cites gradually decayed until this culture became widely spread throughout a large number of small agricultural communities. This view seems to be supported by recent discoveries such as those at the Harappan site at Pirak near the Nari River in present-day Pakistan. It appears that this settlement was continuously populated from 1800 BCE until the region was occupied by the forces of Alexander the Great in 325 BCE.

When the Vedic culture began to emerge in the Punjab around 1200 BCE with its own distinctive language, ideology, and social order supported by the emergence of new technologies including advanced metallurgy and glass production, it swept aside, supplanted, and absorbed the fragmented remains of the Indus Valley Civilization. By the sixth century BCE, 16 great kingdoms, the Mahājanapadas, dominated present-day India and had begun to create their own large cities. By that time, the Indus Valley Civilization had been all but forgotten, and it would remain so until the discovery of large numbers of bricks by Victorian railway builders.

Conclusion

The Indus Valley Civilization is unique amongst the ancient civilization for several reasons. First and most notably, it seems to have controlled a vast swathe of territory in present-day India and Pakistan but somehow did so without having a large army or by conquering other, weaker cultures. Almost every other equivalent civilization was created through conquest and by military power.

The cities of this culture were very different too. Unlike almost every other ancient city, these did not develop organically over time in a random way. Instead, they were carefully planned and featured sophisticated sanitation and waste-disposal systems around 4,000 years before such things became common in Europe.

The Indus Valley Civilization developed advanced metallurgy, medicine, and dentistry, the accurate measurement of size, weight, and time, used wheeled vehicles, and what were at the time some of the largest cities in the world. Yet they seem to have done this without a single ruler such as a monarch or emperor. Many people use this culture as an example of a truly egalitarian society which prospered without an autocratic ruler or the need for large armies.

Then, the Indus Valley Civilization gradually went into decline and finally disappeared. Even its memory was lost until British archaeologists became curious about the piles of mud bricks which were being discovered in the plains of the Punjab.

The Indus Valley Civilization is one of the most significant, extensive, and most influential of all the ancient civilizations, yet it is one about which we still know relatively little. Our understanding of this culture is evolving, and it seems likely that there is still a great deal to be discovered about the mysterious Indus people.

Made in the USA
Columbia, SC
21 June 2025